Seven Secrets of Successful Fundraising

A Handbook for Both the Professional and New Fundraiser

Amal Abdalhakim-Douglas

Black Stone Press & DMC Books

ISBN: 978-0-9535993-4-9

http://www.amaldouglas.com

http://www.black-stone.net/books

CONTENTS

Author's Preface

One of the people this book is written for is the kind of person (a bit like myself) who once they get some good advice or tips on how to improve what they are doing, try to implement it straight away. However, it will also most certainly benefit those who like to keep some useful books like a dictionary or other reference material close to hand so that they can refer to it at the appropriate time.

My involvement in teaching and supporting educational projects is probably a good place to talk about my fundraising background. For although this often involved seeking commercial sponsorship, writing grant applications, face to face soliciting, selling tickets, fundraising events, written appeals and more. In my mind these were just things one had to do. So for 20 years I've been fundraising and supporting social enterprise before the phrase was even invented.

It's all helped make me a pretty decent fundraiser and a popular fundraising consultant. It's also given me the opportunity develop and deliver some great training sessions that I thoroughly enjoy, and by all accounts so do the delegates who attend. So through this book I'm going to share with you some of the old and newer great secrets I've learned and implemented over the years.

SECRET #1

Build a Winning Fundraising Team

I've trained or spoken to hundreds, if not thousands, of professional fundraisers, dedicated amateurs and eager but unprepared would-be fundraisers. One problem that cuts across the board and often prevents so many from being successful in the first place, or even more successful in the long term, is that they work as individuals. These people have not been able to develop or harness a working and winning team together, meaning they neither see, nor address the very necessary 'wider picture' that is needed for spectacular and sustainable fundraising results.

Even I, despite my experience, sometimes find myself falling into the trap of shooting off a grant applications for a project I'm supporting, that although it may have a very high likelihood of success, would still have benefitted by input from the right person at some stage in the process.

Many academics and scholars working in the business sector have attempted to analyse different 'types' of people for various reasons, Belkin and Honey & Mumford (perhaps the best known in fundraising circles) amongst them. These various philosophies or techniques may in many cases be loosely based or influenced by the principles of Yin and Yang, the elements (earth, water, fire air), studies relating to the various sections of the brain (left, right, front back), signs of the zodiac or traditional healing categories (hot, cold, wet, dry). Having looked in depth at many of these things myself I'm convinced that they each have something to offer in different circumstances, Perhaps the best lesson is simply that the "one size fits all" way of thinking does not work in fundraising,

In both this and the following chapter I'm going to take you through an exercise that is an integral part of my workshops. On every occasion that I run this exercise I can guarantee that at least one person will announce that it was worth attending and paying the asking price just for that one session alone, and all this before the first mid-morning coffee break.

To start you'll have to complete my Working Styles Questionnaire, which is in fact a self-survey and definitely not a test, as there are no right or wrong answers and no scoring.

All that is required of you is to be as honest as possible in looking at twenty questions or statements, and ticking the seven that you either **most agree with**, or that **reflect you** or your thoughts most accurately.

figure 1: Hajj Amal's Working Styles Questionnaire

Tick the SEVEN phrases that you either agree with most, or they most reflect you.

[1] My reports tend to be shorter and more direct than anyone else's.

[2] I find using analysis techniques to be generally very useful.

[3] I don't appreciate people who rush into things without adequate preparation.

[4] I get frustrated with people who don't adopt a logical approach.

[5] I don't like people who are too quiet in meetings, I prefer them to air their views.

[6] I regularly seek out new thrills, trying things I've not done before.

[7] When I present a report it will MORE LIKELY be the third draft than the first.

[8] I don't tend to socialise with my colleagues a lot, I prefer keeping things on a formal and professional basis.

[9] The most important thing is that it 'works in practice.'

[10] People often dwell too much on mistakes or failures instead of moving on.

[11] I like to work to clear structures and guidelines.

[12] I generally prefer to wait until all the facts are known before I act.

[13] People DO NOT tend to describe me as tactful.

[14] I tend to be one of the most talkative in meetings.

[15] I'm NOT keen on people who are flippant or happy-go-lucky.

[16] Too little time allocated to tasks is a MAJOR reason for failure.

[17] In discussions I'm the one UNLIKELY to become passionate either for or against any particular position or suggestion.

[18] I tend to be one of the LEAST talkative in meetings.

[19] I DON'T like when people digress from the subject in hand.

[20] Many great ideas come from spontaneous brainstorming sessions.

NB. Make sure you have ***only ticked seven*** *questions or statements*

The next step requires that on the pie chart opposite you shade in the numbered sections or segments that correspond with the questions or statements you ticked on the Working Styles Questionnaire.

figure 2: Working Styles Pie Chart

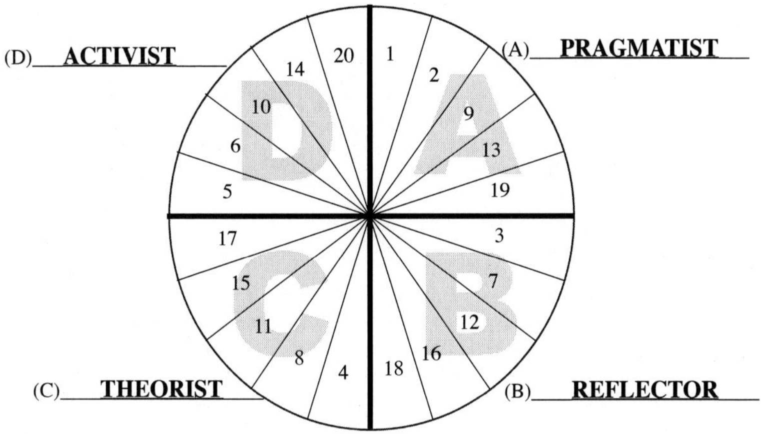

So what does this all mean?

If you scored heaviest (i.e. shaded more) in **Section A**, then in terms of your working style you're probably what we would call a **Pragmatist**.

If you scored heaviest in **Section B**, then in terms of your working style you're probably what we would call a **Reflector.**

If you scored heaviest in **Section C**, then in terms of your working style you're probably what we would call a **Theorist.**

If you scored heaviest in **Section D** then in terms of your working style you're probably what we would call an **Activist.**

Before we look at the implications of each working style you have to firstly remember that this is not an exact science. Secondly, a lot depends on the frankness and honesty of how the questionnaire was answered. Thirdly, in my experience those who protests the loudest that they are definitely not a Reflector, Activist, Pragmatist or Theorist are in most cases unanimously seen by their colleagues as exactly that.

If you are a PRAGMATIST you are probably already wondering "what's the point of this exercise" and will this be of practical use in your fundraising. You like to cut to the chase and are not to keen on lots of meaningless theoretical exercises. The great thing is that you'll keep things focussed while others are floundering.

The negative side is that if you don't see something as useful or practical you're likely to switch off, much to the annoyance of your colleagues. This also means that your solutions or completed jobs may sometimes not be as beneficial to others as you might often think, as they have not addressed a particular point or issue that others may consider to be of major importance or fundamental to the process.

If you are a REFLECTOR you don't want to be rushed. You'll have been one of the last to finish this exercise simply because you want to make sure that you have definitely picked the right seven statements to tick (which of course means you want to get the most out of the exercise). You'll make sure you've read the contract before signing and that you've checked the figures before signing off on the report. Your analysis, questioning and attention to detail will have saved many people from making costly or embarrassing mistakes.

Of course the other side is that you may often be the one "holding up the process" by seeking to analyse and reflect on things that everybody else is absolutely clear about. You'll be considered to slow and indecisive when action is needed and perhaps a spoilsport by not wanting to engage in things like role play or scenario simulation when others see it as a great learning or preparation tool. If in a senior position, your reluctance to take the helm or be decisive in a time of crisis may also leave you open to criticism.

If you are a THEORIST you're probably someone who naturally inclines to what is often described as 'lateral thinking." You'll take all the components and be able to streamline them into a clear course of action, or even paint the bigger and more comprehensive picture. You'll appreciate decisions based on a clear logical or defined scoring system and don't like when the "goal posts are moved." You're good at getting yourself focussed on the matter at hand and getting to the root of the question, "why?" Colleagues may gravitate to you when they've been given a task and don't quite know where to start.

The downside is that your real or perceived lack of emotional attachment may not endear others to working with you. You'll also likely procrastinate in terms of decision making because you feel you've not been given enough to work with (contrary to everyone else's opinion). You may inadvertently belittle colleagues by constantly displaying your intolerance for their lack of grasping or working to what you see as clear guidelines or principles.

If you are an ACTIVIST you're probably not surprised, as you like brainstorming, facing new challenges and taking the lead when necessary. Definitely more Yang than Yin, so not one keen on writing up reports or having to do a lot of reading or research before making a decision. People will gravitate to you in order to bounce exciting new ideas around. They also know you won't be afraid to "get your hands dirty" and back them up when the going gets tough.

The problem is that you may well be known by others as someone likely to act first and think later, leave things half finished or be someone who doesn't considers all the possible consequences before embarking on a course of action, "shooting from the hip," as it were. Your colleagues may also regard you as someone much too focussed on being the centre of attention.

I'm pretty certain that some of you will not be too pleased with these definitions or conclusions. Some of you will say it's pretty fair and accurate. Some may be in denial, and some may even be baying for my blood and saying it's a load of old poppycock (if not something far worse). However, despite that, you will still have learned a very important lesson, in that not everybody thinks or works in the same way that you do.

The most important point to learn here is that to have an effective team you need all of these four elements. It's also good to know that whatever you came out as is probably how your colleagues actually perceive you, even if you don't recognise some of those traits in yourself. However, in order to complete this very first and important *secret* we'll come back and add the finishing touches in chapter 3.

I hope you will have realised that whatever your working style, it has its positives, but you also have to be on guard to make sure you don't slip into the negative side of your working style. If that negative slide is already noticeable then you need to take steps to gradually correct that behaviour and begin to put things right.

As you move through the chapters this will all begin to make even more sense as we now begin to approach fundraising in earnest.

SECRET #2

Understand the Fundraising Cycle

I keep six honest serving men
(They taught me all I knew)
Their names are What and Why and When
And Where and How and Who
(Rudyard Kipling)

The Working Styles Analysis is something that can be used in building an effective team in just about any type of organisation or around any kind of projects. However, what will be addressed in this chapter is something that is quite specific to fundraising. In fact, it's relevant to each and every fundraising drive, whether a major donor campaign, grant application or fundraising event, namely the **'fundraising cycle.'**

Everything in the fundraising cycle is effectively leading up to "**The Ask.**" In other words looking at those very points indicated by Rudyard Kipling in his poem above:

- **What** to ask for?
- **How** to ask?
- **Who** to ask?

- **Where** to ask?
- **When** to ask? and even
- **Why** to ask?

The fundraising cycle is a clear, workable, sustainable and proven system for addressing these matters effectively, no matter what the size, scope or individual quirks of the fundraising campaign. This is applicable whether you want to raise hundreds, hundreds of thousands or millions of pounds, euros or dollars.

You will see from the following graphical representation that the fundraising cycle is divided into four separate components.

- Establishing the Case for Support;
- Segmentation & Research;
- Development of the Plan;
- Monitoring & Evaluation.

figure 3: The Fundraising Cycle

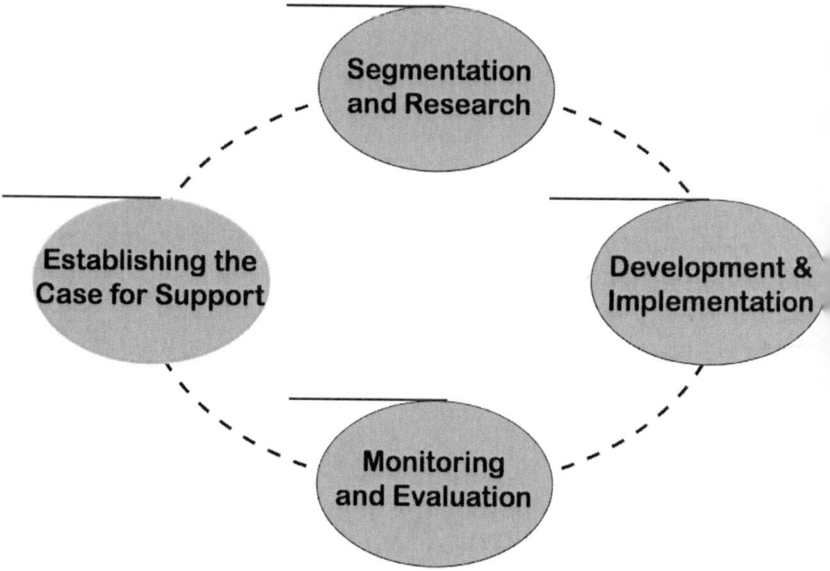

Establishing the Case for Support

This is often thought to be the first point on the cycle but the truth, as you will see, is that you can actually start anywhere on the cycle. I like to start with the case for support because it is for many the easiest one of the four to grasp, and the one that many fundraisers may already have some familiarity with.

What you are really doing is collating all the information that will allow the project to be described clearly, which means identifying the beneficiaries, the benefits and the expected or desired outcomes. You will need to show proof that the project is needed and possibly gain endorsements from supporters and potential partners.

Many will have heard the story of the man who swept the floor at NASA, when asked what he does for a living, he replied "I help to send astronauts into space."

Similarly the person involved in establishing the case for support doesn't just say *"we want to run a five -a-side football competition."* He wants to "*raise the esteem of young people, promote health & fitness and reduce street crime by organising and hosting a football competition involving local young people who are unemployed, not in mainstream education or facing disadvantage"*

So in order to be able to do this you must already know who the beneficiaries are, what the outcomes should be, the nature of the project to be delivered and perhaps more importantly, all the reasons why the project is needed.

Segmentation and Research

Logically this follows on from establishing the case for support. The job here is to produce an analysis of target beneficiaries, all relevant demographic information, technical information, relevant statistics, case studies, a profile of target donors and the best methods to communicate with each of them.

In other words the person conducting the segmentation and research will know that we should be targeting *"professionals between the ages of 25 and 40, who live locally, and might be sports fans."* He (or she for that matter) will work out that the place to target these people may be the local train station and recommend ways of getting the desired message to them. They may suggest a poster campaign at the station or an advertisement in the free newspaper given to commuters. That person will also identify and evaluate different sources of funding while also being up to date on how similar projects have been funded in the past. They will also project the likely yield from each target donor group or from each possible fundraising method to be employed.

If starting at this point on the cycle then the job might be more focussed on finding out how the organisation is perceived externally. This includes discovering who is most likely to support the organisations work in general and how these target groups are motivated. A key principle will be understanding the dynamics of the fundraising pyramid *(see page 69)*. This is a graphical representation which suggests that in many major donor fundraising campaigns the likelihood is that 80% of funds received will come from 20% of your donors and conversely, the other 20% from the remaining 80% of donors.

Development of the Plan

If the person responsible for Development of the Plan has been informed of what to ask for, who to ask, and of course how and when to ask, then he has everything he needs in order to get to work.

He can now begin to look at and allocate all the necessary resources to make it all happen and come up with a clear plan of action that will have targets and timeframes that include preparation of materials, allocation of specific jobs and other staffing details. He'll be able to say *"we need three telesales staff, an office two phone lines and 5,000 posters"* and also be able to say when and how the posters will be distributed.

If starting here, it may be a case of making sure that everything is in place to hit the fundraising trail once a suitable project has been given the green light. This may be in terms of staffing, generic fundraising materials, and the correct corporate profile *(see chapter 8)*.

Monitoring and Evaluation

This involves getting to grips with what really happened after a plan has been developed and put into action. You will have to make the effort to really understand what was successful or viable and what was not, in terms of demographic profile, methods used, the case for support and the management and execution of all the component parts. This all gets fed back into the cycle. Questions that will have to be answered include:

> *"Was it the right target audience?*
>
> *Was the target audience reached effectively?*
>
> *Did the method of engagement work?*
>
> *Were resources deployed effectively?"*

These same findings are those that can be used to develop feedback to donors in order to keep them informed, and with a view to building long term fruitful relationships.

Of course an effective way to start any fundraising is to

have effective monitoring and evaluation of what has occurred previously. So again it confirms that you can start the fundraising cycle at any point.

We're not quite done on this topic yet, but certainly don't be tempted to down-play the significance of each phase of the Fundraising Cycle in **any and every** fundraising campaign. If you've grasped everything so far, we're now ready to start pulling the strands together in terms of making you a more effective fundraiser.

SECRET #1 PART 2

Put Your Winning Team to Work

We now have our first piece of cross-referencing as we pull together the work covered in both chapters 1 and 2. Most people will have scored heavily in one working style but also scored in at least one other as none of us are completely one-dimensional. However it has been observed that people with a certain working styles are more likely to have an aptitude to particular types of work.

Go back to the fundraising cycle graphic on page 9 and you will see that there is a line above each point on the cycle. On each of those lines you need to write as follows:

Above "Monitoring & Evaluation" write **REFLECTOR**

Above "Development of the Plan" write **PRAGMATIST**

Above "Segmentation & Research" write **THEORIST**

Above "Establishing the Case for Support" write **ACTIVIST**

On the following page we've actually done it for you.

figure 4: The Fundraising Cycle - Amended

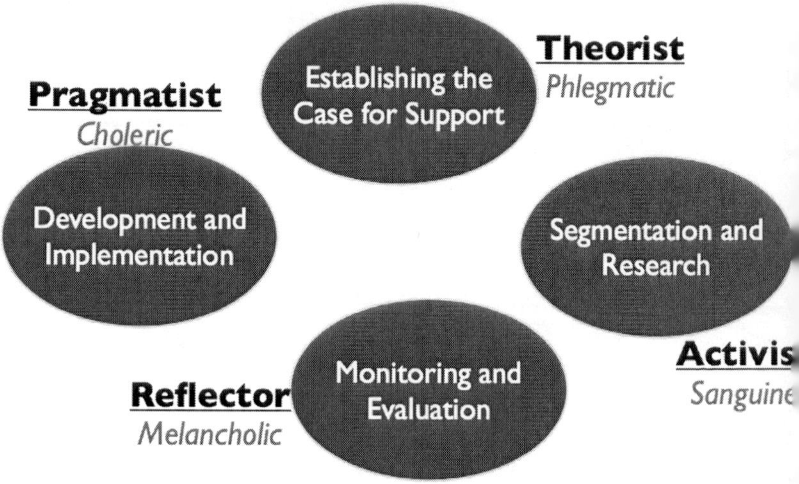

Now in my live workshops this is where individual delegates go "ooh" and the proverbial penny starts to drop. For this explains why so many solo fundraisers find it so easy to start the process and then get bogged down at the precise time when things should be moving on in leaps and bounds.

As a fundraiser it's imperative that you develop a team that consists of all these varied types of people, thus ensuring each part of the cycle is effectively addressed.

Now, in establishing your team you really do have to *think outside the box*. If you work in a larger organisation then pull in a lady from marketing, a guy from accounts and an old-hand working at the coal-face delivering the projects to beneficiaries, and you definitely have to make use of trustees and directors. In a smaller organisation or if you are a freelancer then make reciprocal arrangements with other fundraisers to look over each others proposals, funding strategies and projects.

It may well be that you or someone else needs to move away from establishing the case for support and concentrate on monitoring and evaluation, while another person needs to concentrate on segmentation and research while pulling someone else into developing the plan.

Of course it could well be that you really are the person best placed to address more than one part of the fundraising cycle. In fact as a professional fundraiser it's even possible that three or even all four parts of the process are best addressed by you.

DON'T KID YOURSELF...

...That's a recipe for disaster and would mean you've just wasted a lot of time in taking up and reading this book. The other trap to avoid is belittling any part of the fundraising cycle and relegating it to being less important than another, simply because you can't get your head around it. Believe me, someone else you know can, and when they do you'll appreciate the difference.

So now hopefully you will see that you need other people (who are not necessarily like you) to be part of the fundraising team. Perhaps you'll also begin to appreciate some of your existing colleagues that little bit more.

You now have the first two great secrets that will allow

you to get out there and approach your fundraising in a completely new way, with a much better chance of success. You have an idea of the team you need to build and precisely where these skills need to be deployed and put into practice.

So in order to earn your first coffee break you now have to turn to page 85 and make a list of colleagues or other people you know (and who you will actively seek out) in order to discuss this process with them and thus keep things moving forward.

SECRET #3

Explore Different Fundraising Options

A common problem for those responsible for fundraising is often a tendency to rely solely on one type or method of fundraising for everything. This may manifest itself in an over-reliance on grant applications, fundraising dinners or gifts from a particular set of donors or supporters. Diversifying the fundraising strategy not only increases the possible options, but allows a completely new set of people to become involved in the fundraising process, new skills to be developed and stops good strategies being wasted on the wrong projects.

At this point in our 'Seven Secrets of Fundraising" workshops I like to ask delegates to throw out as many types of fundraising methods they can think of. So you should do the same. Turn to page 85 and in two minutes write down as many ways of fundraising as you can, starting with the ones you have already used at one time or another.

Now if your list is of less than five then you've lived a very sheltered fundraising life. This does not necessarily mean you've not been successful, but on the other hand, if you're a professional fundraising consultant then perhaps you should worry. Despite that, even a list of over 20 may signify a lot of experience, but let's hope it's not a result of always chopping and changing due to a constant lack of success. Remember the saying, *Jack of All Trades.... Master of None.*

I generally list around 20 and find that after that most things can fit into one of the already mentioned categories. So what I'll do is mention a few of them here under around fifteen different headings. I will then give a short explanation of each. I'll follow this with a tip based on the most common real-life questions I get from delegates attending the live workshops, or via email from listeners of the Consultant's View podcast.

Private or Personal Funds - Bootstrapping

Quite often the first port of call for new or small organisations. Individuals see a social or charitable need and address it in the first instance by using their own funds, time and energy. However, after some time they realise this is often unsustainable unless they are quite wealthy individuals and also have a lot of time on their hands. In this category we also include money from family and close friends.

Top Tip: *If you do use your own money then be clear from the outset to either record it as (i) a grant, in which case you are building up the track record of the organisation in receiving grants. or (ii) a loan, in which case when money does come in from other sources, you'll be entitled to reimburse yourself by repaying the loan.*

Loans

Of course the main problem with loans is that you have to pay them back, and unfortunately raising funds to pay off debts can be a very hard thing to do. In addition, normally to receive a loan you would have to demonstrate that you are very likely to have the means to repay it in the future. Meaning that the charity or project will have to be shown to be either receiving income from trading activity or have been promised a gift or donations which can be verified, along with the donors consent for their gift to be used for loan repayment.

Top Tip: *If possible offer lenders the opportunity to turn loans into Service Level Agreements (SLAs) or sponsorship deals, if you can actually offer the lender a benefit such as free advice, expertise or branding of some sort. This will also mean the lender has a vested interest in promoting the organisation and keeping it successful.*

Investment Funds

Similarly, investment funds will only work if you are likely to produce a profit, as with a social enterprise. However, having investors is fraught with danger and in some instances would mean not being recognised as a charitable cause, even if the investment is small. If there is a need for a commercial type relationship then perhaps offering a commission on sales or training fees (for referring customers) would be preferable. However, offering commission for fundraising itself is an altogether different proposition which in my opinion should generally be avoided or at least approached with great caution. It is also not encouraged by the Institute of Fundraising and other bodies.

Top Tip: *The commission route is definitely the better option and means the investor has a vested interest in your success. A time limit should be included in any contract.*

Gifts & Donations

This is the real bread and butter stuff of many organisations and the key to this is to keep the charity or project in the eye of the public (or at least in the eye of target donors) so that when they do want to give, you're the first in line. In my opinion people are always willing and seeking to give to charitable causes and you simply have to make it easy for them. Schools, social groups, families, marathon runners, celebrities and thrill seekers are always looking to support a worthy cause so it's imperative you keep your cause noticed and on their respective radars.

Top Tip: *If you are a registered UK charity don't forget to sign up for Gift Aid and adjust any sponsorship or donation forms or webpages appropriately. Also be sure that you have and use a Generic Fundraising Statement (see the following chapter) on all printed or published materials.*

Legacies

This is the major source of funding for charities in the UK (animal charities in particular) yet one of the hardest to plan for. Of course, as distasteful as it may seem, you could always approach every elderly, frail or sick person you know and try and persuade them to put your project or organisation in their will. However, the truth is that a high percentage of legacies are received from benefactors the organisation has never heard of prior to receiving the gift. Despite this, leaving information in solicitors offices and being listed in charity directories and strategic or high profile websites are some of the things that can be done that traditionally yield results over time.

Top Tip: *A carefully worded, well printed and very personalised letter sent to targeted individuals might not only in the long term yield results, but also the likelihood is that many would respond with an immediate donation should the right "buttons" be pressed.*

Profits from Trading

This is becoming increasingly popular through charity shops and the internet in particular, and seems (at the moment, anyway) to also be supported by government structures as the social enterprise model becomes more prevalent. However, it may require checking or even changing your constitution to ensure that the organisation is actually legally able to trade.

Top Tip: *Having volunteers manning the shop or the internet may save some money, but ultimately if you are running a business, you need to have a serious business-minded person in charge.*

Sponsorship

With CSR (Corporate Social Responsibility) being a recurring flavour of the day it's a good time to put pressure on big business to support local charitable work. In this instance you have to remember that it cuts both ways, they also want something. The task here involves putting together a clear package of benefits which might include advertisements or their logo on all your printed materials, a recruitment stand at your event, an award in their name, or perhaps a logo on an item you have purchased. Health/ medical and childrens charities have traditionally been the main beneficiaries of this type of support. However, this area is one of the first to be affected by any downturn in the economy so that should always be borne in mind.

Top Tip: *Two important points. (i) You may be a charitable cause but they're not, they are a business and this is a business deal, so learn to talk in a businesslike manner at the right times. (ii) Make sure you continually push to be having conversations with a person as high up in the targeted company as possible, but without stepping on the toes of the person who may have got you inside in the first place.*

Grants

Whether from government or a private grant-making institution, in most cases the process is the same. The body advertises what they will give grants for, what the process is and any relevant timeframes or dates. Applicants normally fill in a form supplied by the potential funder and submit it along with supporting documentation. It's probable that yours will be one of many applications under consideration and that many will be unsuccessful based on either the funders priorities at that time or just simply the sheer volume of applications received, chasing a limited amount of cash.

Top Tip: *If you can't come to a "Seven Secrets of Fundraising" workshop then pay special attention to the following chapter on submitting great grant applications.*

Payroll Giving & Gift Aid

Generally both these (along with legacies and share giving) are included under the umbrella of "Tax Effective Giving" In the UK they are governed by HMRC (Revenue & Customs).

Payroll Giving is a method of getting employees to have a sum taken out of their wages before tax and contributed to your cause. The government then add the employees saved tax to your donation. So for example, for a charity to receive £10, a payroll donor may only have to give around £7.80 and the government will make up the rest.

Gift Aid is a system where the government via HMRC will add a certain amount to any cash donations or gifts you receive that fit their criteria. At the time of writing it works out to an additional 38p for every £1 donated. Once you are signed up to the scheme you have to ensure that donors (a) choose to opt in to have their donation gift aided, (b) list their address including the postcode, and (c) verify that they are a UK taxpayer.

Top Tip: *Visit the HMRC website for more information, but the trick (particularly with payroll giving) is to make sure the targeted company has opted into the scheme and then get in front of as many employees as possible as they also have to "choose" to both opt into the scheme and also make you the beneficiary.*

Dues, Subscriptions & Membership Fees

A great many organisations exist solely on this type of income. What you don't want to do is take advantage of supporters by taking their money and offering them nothing in return. The fact is that happy and paid up members are the first people likely to give you more when new campaigns are launched or the organisation is in a temporary financial bind. They are also often a conduit to much bigger donors to come on board. Sports clubs often make a paid membership fee a prerequisite to team selection. Other common benefits include a newsletter, cheaper or free entry to events, the right to vote on particular matters or some other preferential treatment that the organisation is in a position to bestow.

Top Tip: *Try and work with local businesses to get them to permanently offer members attractive discounts. It may require producing plastic (dated) membership cards but the extra you can charge should more than compensate.*

Sub contracts

Although charities and voluntary organisations are being encouraged down this route, I consider it a bit of a red herring. Unfortunately a lot of time is now spent in the voluntary sector chasing delivery contracts. It's true that these organisations often have great expertise amongst their members and staff but this needs to be delivered on their own terms. Also, winning a contract often has the effect of significantly changing the outlook of an organisation and moving it away from its core objectives or original target beneficiaries.

The positive side of sub-contracting is that it is a way of easily allowing organisations to work together and share expertise. I'm definitely an advocate of a number of charitable organisations coming together to form a joint training organisation that they all contribute to and benefit from. In my time I've helped set-up a number of these entities.

Top Tip: *Think long and hard about going down this route and delegate one person to follow through on leads in this area.*

Consultancy & Training

Again, charitable organisations have often built up a huge expertise and method of delivery to the people that matter. It therefore makes sense to offer that expertise to those willing to pay for it. In many instances this is an opportunity for volunteers to legitimately earn some money and thus be in a position to keep volunteering. It also allows an organisation to build up its resumé and thus be a more attractive option for future funding.

Top Tip: *Draw on the expertise within your organisation to develop a few key modules that all sectors (public, private and voluntary) can use in their own delivery or training programmes. Advertise it on websites and other literature and include it in sponsorship deals and membership benefits.*

Door to Door

Very traditional form of fundraising that can be surprisingly effective and is making a comeback. However, you must ensure that any teams sent out are effectively trained and aware of any legal and ethical issues. A good place for guidance is the Institute of Fundraising website. You may also need permission from local authorities.

Top Tip: *If in doubt about using someone as a rep' then* ***don't*** *use them. Any bad publicity will multiply a hundredfold on a small or medium sized charity, particularly in the local context. Although there is no harm in revisiting potential donors at a later date make sure you are aware of who has already given, and pop in to say thank you or hand deliver an update or newsletter.*

Street Collections

Both this and Door to Door could be classified as **Face to Face Fundraising**, again, local government permission will probably be necessary and there are some clear guidelines that have to be followed. For example rattling a tin is these days seen as an act of intimidation and has to be avoided. Again, the Institute of Fundraising website is a good place to check.

Top Tip: *Some big national charities engage in this and are very good at it. So watch them closely in terms of their approach, the people they use, the locations they choose, the number of collectors and what they actually ask for from people they stop.*

Internet/Online

This of course assumes that any serious voluntary sector organisation or project will at least have a basic website. Firstly, you must make it absolutely clear on the website that you are seeking and willingly accept donations (more about this in the next chapter).This is where the generic fundraising statement comes in. This is the phrase or clause that everyone knows and that makes it very clear why people should give you money. After that you then have to make it easy for people to donate such as via a paypal donate button. You also need to use this opportunity to collect as much information as possible from the donor in order to build a donor profile and add them to your database for future fundraising campaigns.

Top Tip: *Use the expertise within your organisation to have a blog and/or podcast series that drives traffic to* *the site but that also works directly as a fundraising tool via the content itself. Additionally, see the chapters in this book on developing a Generic Fundraising Statement and Developing the Database.*

Auctions, Dinners & Other Fundraising Events

This is the fastest growing area in terms of charity income, as with the growth of reality TV shows and the like, people now want to be involved in the experience. Events are great showcases and can be harnessed for long term publicity as well as short to medium term fundraising. A point to remember is that the people involved in organising or marketing the fundraising event must believe in it and have an empathy with the target donors. So if you are auctioning a £20 bottle of wine but expecting to get £1,000, or selling dinner places at £500 a ticket, then definitely avoid having someone doing the selling who is appalled at such extravagance.

You should certainly not feel compelled to invite the very people you are trying to help (who may in fact be at the opposite end of the social scale at least in monetary terms) unless it's for one of them to thank everyone for their contributions and encourage more. Very important to also ensure you work with the press as there is a lot of leverage to be had from a good relationship.

Top Tip: *(i) Every step of the process is a fundraising campaign in itself. This involves getting venues paid for, obtaining products and services to auction, getting people and organisations to advertise via their own networks, soliciting patronage, engaging entertainers, special guests and professional auctioneers. A successful event* ***starts***

with not having to pay for any of these things, meaning all income goes to the cause. (ii) There are many thrill seekers out there looking for a reason to justify their desire to bungee jump of a mountain or run a marathon for a worthy cause. Not only that, but they'll pay for the privilege and get additional sponsorship to boot.

Of course this is not an exhaustive list and the beauty of fundraising is that you'll always hear of something new that's worked for somebody else, or someone putting a new twist to an old favourite.

I know I haven't mentioned **direct mail** or **personal visits** to potential high donors, **press advertising**, **telephone fundraising** or the **annual calendar**, but the list can literally go on and on, and I do mention some of these other things at other points in the book or more specifically in other publications.

Crucially you must remember that the fundraising cycle applies no matter what form of fundraising you use. You must establish a case for support. You must segment and research. You must develop the delivery plan. You must monitor and evaluate.

Somehow you have to find a way of repeatedly feeding all these possible fundraising methods into the mix to see when it becomes possible to use one of them for a particular project, even if it's not the main means you intend to employ.

SECRET #4

Develop a Generic Fundraising Statement

Be honest! Why should anyone give money to your organisation?

Come on! Turn to page 86 and write a short concise answer!

Now, if you were able to give a short concise answer then that was probably your **generic fundraising statement**. A clear reason why your organisation is worth supporting and giving money to.

The Generic Fundraising Statement is that statement that once heard has the effect of people immediately dipping into their pockets and donating to your cause. The great thing about money generated in this way is that it will be unrestricted, meaning not tied to any particular project and so can be used for general overheads or core work.

For successful fundraising to take place it is important that everyone involved in an organisation is aware of, and able to articulate, the ***generic fundraising statement*** which should reflect the prior and much more comprehensive

generic case for support which sits alongside the business plan. This is exactly the same as everyone knowing the phone number, postal address or website address and should be viewed and accepted as such.

As a charitable organisation you have need to have absolute clarity on three things

(i) What you actually do or were set up to do;

(ii) Who benefits;

(iii) How they benefit.

In an earlier example I mentioned the man who swept the floor at NASA who when asked what he does for a living, replied, "I help to send astronauts into space." Similarly the Generic Fundraising Statement makes it clear who benefits from your work and what problem you are tackling.

For example something like *"helping people out of the poverty trap"* or *"providing life experiences for people with cerebral palsy"* or *"using your donations to help victims of war."* They don't necessarily have to be as short as that, but for the 'statement' you want something that is memorable, has a strong impact and can be easily used on websites, stationery and all printed materials, and perhaps even as part of a logo.

The aim is to make sure that the person reading or hearing the statement is in no doubt that you are in need of donations, and that the money will be well spent. So the key things to try and get into a statement are the benefits, the beneficiaries and how you work.

A good exercise to do in generating a generic fundraising

statement is first of all to look for great examples via websites and publications and then to gather together individuals with varying connections to the organisation (e.g., trustees, staff, volunteers, beneficiaries) and put certain questions to each of them, demanding a list of their top three one word (or short phrase) answers to each. Questions might include:

- Where do we operate?
- Who do we serve (and who do we work with)?
- What do we do?
- What benefits do those we serve get?

A correlation of the top words might give an indication of what might be in your statement. For example if the following came up as the most common to the four questions; **Scotland, Disabled, Trips, Experience**, then a first draft of a generic fundraising statement might read something like. *"Helping Scotland's disabled community sample life changing experiences through day trips and excursions"*

You can see how something like that could be re-drafted a few times before making it totally your own. Why not have a go at re-drafting your own. I'm always willing to take a look and add a few suggestions. Just drop me an email.

I haven't put much emphasis on the much larger and comprehensive *Generic Case for Support*. For in practice it is the shorter statement and the work involved in developing that statement that will have an immediate impact on staff, volunteers and potential donors.

SECRET #5

Submit Great Grant Applications

For some organisations written grant applications may be the only form of fundraising they engage in. This may be because they are connected to an umbrella organisation that has traditionally given them grant aid. Or they were perhaps originally set up with a gift from a grant-making institution which continues to offer support in this way. Sometimes its just the easiest method of fundraising those involved with the project are comfortable with, and probably the one that has been most successful.

However, total reliance on grant aid is fraught with danger, as a change in policy by a funder could result in a 100%, and thus un-survivable, drop in income. The other problem is that in many instances grants tend to be given for projects outside of an organisation's normal line of work which is not always desirable.

I'm often asked what is a large grant and what's a small grant. The truth is that it depends who's asking. For an organisation that's had an average income of £10,000 for the last three years £50,000 might be considered large. However, for my local theatre that recently finished a £10,000,000 (that's £10 million) campaign then it might barely get a mention. Of course it also depends very much on the donor. If it's coming out of my own pocket then I would consider giving a donation of £50,000 to any cause to be a lot of money. However, If it's coming from the European Union it might simply be taken out of "petty cash."

I'll start by looking at five things you need to be aware of when applying for grants and then take you through some of the key questions you'll probably have to answer on any grant application form, whether it be from a private trust, government body, lottery fund or European source.

The first and most important thing that you absolutely must do in dealing with grant applications is **read thoroughly the guidelines of the funding body** and look at its funding history in terms of projects and organisations it has supported in the past.

Also be sure to look for any reports and research that they may have sponsored or published, as your work may well fit into one of the recommendations from such a report which would be a big bonus. So make sure you clearly point out that your project fulfils what was recommended in that report.

FIVE THINGS YOU NEED TO KNOW WHEN APPLYING FOR GRANT FUNDING

i) WHO CAN APPLY FOR GRANT FUNDING:

Who can apply depends solely on the stipulations set out by the grant making body.

- **Registered charities** are the one entity that almost everyone will fund.

- **Voluntary & community groups** that may have a constitution but not a legal entity such as a registered company or registered charity will often be funded, but only to a certain level. So in other words only up to a small to medium sized grant.

- **Social enterprise** is a name given to a charitable organisation that desires to carry out some form of commercial activity which coincides with its charitable aims, using any proceeds from these activities to support those same aims. As such they will normally be a registered legal entity or a voluntary group with a constitution and the funding eligibility will depend more on the status of the entity than anything else.

- **Religious Organisations**. There are many funding bodies that support a specific faith (particularly Jewish and Christian in the UK) and thus many **faith bodies** successfully apply directly to these organisations for funding their activities. However, outside of that, most funders will not fund what is seen as direct religious activity.

- **Schools.** Whether state run or private (confusingly called public in the UK) Many schools often apply for grant funding. As above, religious schools may actually have a slight advantage in this respect from being able to apply to religious charities. Otherwise it's unusual to get grants for normal educational activities that it is considered should be provided by the state. This also applies to other organisations applying to fund educational activities.

- **Public Sector Bodies**. It's surprising how many **government agencies** actually do apply for and receive private grant funding. This will nearly always be for projects going beyond their normal scope of responsibility and will often be in partnership with another external organisation.

ii) What can grant funding be given for?

Funding can be given for just about any legitimate project cost whether it be salaries, setting up costs, management costs, general overheads professional fees, equipment or other capital expenditure. Again, it all depends on the particular funding body, their rules in place at that time and of course how you justify each particular item of expenditure.

iii) What won't get funding

Almost universally you won't get funding for projects that only benefit one individual (excluding the likes of educational bursaries). It follows that with so many different potential funders they'll each have things they don't like, but some things that come up time and time again include:

- Second-hand vehicles and computers (new is often stipulated)
- General running costs or overheads
- Loan repayments
- Costs incurred before the project started
- Religious activities
- Trade & business activities

Not only should equipment be new but some funds have clear guidelines on what amount they'll give for certain equipment such as computers or cameras meaning you'd have to explain why for example you want £3,000 for a computer when their guideline is £1,650. It may well be that you can explain clearly that it's because of the added and necessary accessories and specialist software which you need for the project. This may readily be accepted as a valid reason.

iv) Reasons for Rejection

Having checked that the organisation is eligible for funding. I'm still amazed at how many applications fall down at the first hurdle. I'm going to layout below some of the most common reasons that I come across as to why grant applications get rejected. Some of them will seem quite obvious yet people fall into these traps time and time again through not paying attention to detail.

- **Not a charitable project:** This in fact often comes down to someone (or a group of people) wanting to set up their own business but confusing the real or perceived benefits customers may receive from their service with "charitable aims."

- **Poorly thought out or presented project:** There is really no excuse for this if you take time to build the team and follow the fundraising cycle outlined in the first chapters of this book and also follow the rest of the guidance in this chapter.

- **No contribution from yourselves** (cash, in kind or match funding): Not always required but project supervision, volunteers time (including trustees) and any office space not being directly charged for, should all be considered and listed as *contributions in-kind*. This shows your commitment to the project.

- **No evidence that the project is needed:** Unfortunately, often overlooked, but don't underestimate the importance of evidence from reports or your own findings showing how much your project is needed. It could come from official reports, news stories, speeches, interviews with target beneficiaries or even personal observations but they must be cited in the proposal.

- **Application does not meet eligibility criteria:** A great project, but you've simply applied to the wrong funder, No doubt because you didn't read their guidelines properly or give them a call just to make sure.

- **Questions answered incorrectly or incompletely:** In most cases if they ask a question they want an answer, and a complete one at that. This is often an indication that there is no teamwork involved here or else it should have been spotted long before the application was submitted.

- **Required information is missing:** As above, go back to chapter 1 and build that fundraising team and then pay attention to Secret number 7.

- **Ineligible constitution or governing document:** Sometimes what's OK for one body is definitely not OK for another. They may object to a clause (or lack thereof), on equal opportunities, the disposal of assets if the organisation is wound up or the way staff or trustees are appointed. If in doubt contact the funder to see if it's alright to send in the governing document (pre-application) for their approval or guidance.

- **Contracts not signed or signed by the wrong person:** Having a dedicated person checking all grant applications before sending will usually catch such omissions.

- **Not enough bank signatories:** Many funders insist that organisations have in place a system that requires more than one signatory to sign cheques or bank withdrawals, They may seek official written confirmation from the bank for this.

- **Unprepared for visit or telephone interview:** People often panic when they get a phone call and say the most stupid things, often contradicting everything they have stated on the application form. The trick is not to get flustered, If you're not ready to talk or don't have a copy of the application form with you then ask the person to call back at a more convenient time. You can even ask them to email you any questions. Quite often its just a small point they want to verify or simply check that you really exist. The same goes for a personal visit. In reality they can find plenty of reasons to reject your application without wasting time on a phone call or personal visit. So a phone call is actually a positive development meaning you've at least cleared the first hurdle.

One of my favourites though not listed here was that "the project was ***too ambitious for the money requested."***

v) Required Documentation

- **Constitution or governing document**: In some instances the charity or company registration numbers may be enough, but quite often they want a signed copy so its good to always have both hard and digital copies available.

- **Bank statements:** Not that often required, but for accounting purposes anyway, you should always have them filed in proper order and easily accessible.

- **Job descriptions:** This applies if you are seeking funding for salaries. You may need to send a detailed job description, **organisation chart** and an explanation of how you arrived at the stated salary (how it compares to similar jobs internally and externally).

- **Latest certified accounts:** Nearly always required. If they are too old they may be rejected, Therefore it's always best to get them completed as soon as possible after the end of the financial year.

- **Full project budget:** Will always be required. Even if the space on the actual form is limited and only able to fit a summary you must always ensure you have a full detailed budget to hand with a breakdown of how every figure was calculated *(e.g. travel expenses = £12 p/week p/person x 6 people x 48 week = £3,456).* It's quite likely that at some point you will be asked to supply the more detailed budget.

- **Letters of endorsement:** Some funders will insist

on getting these sent along with the original application while some may ask for names and contact details, but ask for the actual letters to be sent at a later date. Therefore it makes sense to have them prepared in any case as early as possible and have them sitting down to be brought out when required.

- **Written quotes for goods and services:**

A number of quotes are often demanded for expensive items . A good place to get quotes is via online stores (quoting the URL) as well as known or previously used suppliers. You should ensure that quotes for equipment include delivery charges, installation and warranties as well as the cost of any modifications that may be required (or desired).

ANSWERING THE KEY QUESTIONS

(a) About your group

What you put here will likely never really change from one grant application to another. It's therefore worth spending some time on it and making it known and available to everyone in the organisation along with the generic fundraising statement.

You will need to know:

The date the organisation was established

This might be the date of the first governing document (e.g. Memorandum of Association) or the date when activities started prior to that.

Main aims and objectives

This should be taken from the Constitution, Memorandum of Association or Trust Deed.

Type of Entity

In the UK this will normally be a company limited by guarantee, a registered charity, or voluntary group with a constitution. It may also be an idea to clarify if you are a frontline or 2nd tier delivery organisation.

Contact details

This will include postal address, facsimile number, email address, telephone number and perhaps even something like a skype address and website. You'll also need a contact person who by default should be the Chief Executive or possibly the Chairman, but this last point could be amended to the person responsible for that particular application.

Main activities

This should be your core work and main achievements, but if possible should not be activities that replicate, or are too similar, to the activity you are asking to be funded in a particular grant application.

(b) Describe your project

The space you are given for this may be limited so you have to use it well. You have to also remember that this is your pitch. The first person to read it may well have a hundred of these to go through and their initial decision as to whether you get to the next round will be based on what you've put down here, so get to the point.

In a concise manner you need to try and let them know (1) what problem you are tackling, (2) what the outcomes will be, (3) who the beneficiaries are, (4) what you'll be doing and what the money will be used for. All this while hitting all the buttons of that particular funding scheme, which might be; access to employment or justice, tackling crime or poverty, heritage or sport etc. Here's an example

> *"This project will tackle the issue of exclusion and promote an appreciation of heritage by engaging members of the Somalian, Bosnian and other recent immigrant communities of Cornwall in an oral history project documenting their life experiences. The findings will be shared via the internet, public events and other medium with other residents of Cornwall and further afield. The money will be used to buy audio equipment, training for participants, management costs and developing resources in order to disseminate the results of the project."*

Let's break it down into its component parts:

> **Problem being addressed:** "*...tackle the issue of exclusion...*"
>
> **Beneficiaries:** Those specifically named are members of the Somalian and Bosnian communities and also other residents of Cornwall, although other immigrant communities and people further afield are also mentioned.

Outcomes: Recorded interviews made available via a website as well as , public events (thus bringing people together and tackling exclusion) and "*...promote an appreciation of heritage...*"

Activity: Recording interviews, developing a website and organising events

Expenditure: "*...audio equipment, training for participants, management costs and developing resources...*"

Now let's change the proposed **donor organisation** to one that specifically wants to see **young people** as beneficiaries and the problem of **unemployment** being tackled. Now remember, this is exactly the same project but we just have to show a different side of it.

> *"This project will combat unemployment, lack of skills and anti-social behaviour by giving a group of young people who are either unemployed, not in mainstream education or otherwise disadvantaged, the opportunity to learn new media skills and interact with Cornwall residents they might normally never get to meet, while building up their knowledge of the history of the UK and other countries. This will be done through an oral history project documenting the lives and experiences of members of the Somalian and Bosnian communities of Cornwall and producing CDs, DVD and a website as well as organising public events to showcase the findings and outputs.. The money will be used to buy audio equipment, training for participants, management costs and developing*

resources in order to disseminate the results of the project."

What you need to do right now is think of a project you want to get funding for and make an attempt to write your project description in less than 100 words. The place to start is actually by breaking it down into the component parts. In fact to get that right you really need to re-visit the fundraising cycle and apply the whole process. This means taking it to your team and letting them lose on it. So if you've been paying attention throughout all the chapters you should be ready to have a go and see what you come up with.

Don't forget that if you have attended one of the live workshops or you have paid for a printed or ebook version of this book. Then you can always send me a draft statement via email. I'll personally look over it and send you back my comments and suggestions within a day or two if possible, and I'll keep this open for at least a couple months after purchase *(I don't want to be getting emails five years from now when I'm happily retired).*

(c) Beneficiaries (Who & How Many)

Some funding bodies are very specific about who they want the beneficiaries to be for any project, some are much more flexible in their definitions while some leave it entirely up to you. The catch is that the more freedom you have in choosing your beneficiaries, the more you'll be expected to justify your choice by explaining why and how these people are in need.

Even though you may name specific beneficiaries it's also wise to be as inclusive as possible in the project as a whole. So in the example above the main beneficiaries or target group was very clear (members of the Somalian and Bosnian communities) but other immigrant groups were somehow included as well as the general populace of Cornwall whose lives would also be enriched.

Having worked out who will benefit, you now have to consider the numbers. The assumption is that within reason, the greater number of beneficiaries the better as that's more value for money. Funders know this and they do want numbers, but they are also looking at the actual quality of benefit to be derived by these people. In our example the breakdown of beneficiaries might look something like this:

- Volunteers (experience gained) - 5
- Staff (additional training) - 3
- Participants (those to be interviewed and those working on the technical side) - 24
- Families of participants - 60
- People attending the public events - 200
- People accessing the internet site - 1,500

TOTAL BENEFICIARIES: 1,792

Whatever number you put, make sure you have a complete breakdown (like this example) to hand, so that if you are asked to be more specific you can be.

What you may have to do elsewhere on the application form is explain how you will get these beneficiaries. You'll have to try and demonstrate a track record of working with the target group or a clear recruitment process or partnership with an appropriate other organisation.

(d) Start and finish Dates

Sometimes it may be necessary to break a major project (2 - 5 years) down into smaller sub projects in order to fit some funders criteria (they may not want projects lasting more than a year), while other are quite happy to fund longer term projects that continually build on previous successes and outcomes. As always, you have to read the funders guidelines in terms of the length of projects they are willing to fund or prefer. Also look at previous projects they've funded to see if that gives any clues.

The other important point is the actual start date of the project. You have to speak to someone in the funding organisation or see if they have printed any information on how and when they make decisions. Some will give specific closing dates for applications while some will be open for applications continuously but will state when each round of decisions will be made or what the minimum turnaround time is for decisions on received applications. This means that if it's now March and you want something for the summer and the next meeting is in August you may be wasting your time. Similarly if they state a turnaround time of eight weeks you cannot submit in November an application for a project starting in December.

If you are able to build some flexibility into the project that's a bonus and you may well be asked about that. In other words Month 1 is Month 1, whether that be April, August or December. This of course applies to the finish date as well.

You do need to be aware that some funding programmes have a set date by which all projects must be fully completed. A fully completed project includes any reports and assessments of the project. So make sure you leave adequate time for this within the project timeline and of course make sure you budget for that process as well, as this may include hiring external consultants.

Sometimes, for various reasons, funders have a need to allocate funds to projects. On one occasion I helped three groups respond to an opportunity that required an application to be completed in one day and the project itself completed within six weeks. As far as I remember, one was offered the full amount, one 50% while one was rejected because the first two and a couple of others had been awarded the entire remaining budget left in that kitty. So it's good to have some shorter projects, such as the buying of equipment, always ready to go.

(e) The Budget

There's no golden template for a project budget as each one is unique in time, place and circumstance for both the delivery party and the potential donor. However, a budget that doesn't add up because the maths are wrong is unforgiveable, as is a budget exceeding the limit stipulated by the donor. There is absolutely no excuse for either of these, particularly if you've brought the right people into the fundraising process. You should also remember that the full project budget will normally be higher than the amount you are asking for. This is because you will probably include the value of work done by volunteers, and perhaps the cost of trustees time and even office space which you may not be paying for. These are what we call *contributions in-kind*.

Some donors will even encourage you to add a contingency into the budget (perhaps 5% of the total cost) to cover things like inflation and other unforeseen costs. They don't want to see projects make a great start then get cut short because prices have suddenly increased

Other things to factor in are the additional costs that arise as a result of the application process itself. It is likely that the donor will demand progress reports and a final report on the project. They may also request a change in the proposed outputs or outcomes and all this will need to be negotiated before the final decision. What's important is that you adjust the budget to cover the additional staff costs and overheads required to fulfil these obligations. This may well lengthen the overall duration of the project meaning more management costs. A good donor will prefer to give you the extra money to make sure these things are addressed adequately.

The budget shown on the following pages reflects the actual figures submitted in a grant application for a project that involved taking groups of young people on bicycle tours across the country to visit places of educational and historical interest, The project lasted eighteen months as the organisers wanted to get the benefit of two summers. The maximum grant allowed was £50,000. In my opinion this project represented good value for money. Particularly in that the money was spent largely on the actual activity costs with staffing costs being relatively low.

figure 5: Example of a Project Budget

Equipment

Training Bicycles	£1,200
Computers & software	£1,350
Colour printer	£680
Digital camera	£195
Movie camera hire	£1.000
Camping equipment	£900

Project Leader £4,000

fee for whole project

Administrative Support £3,000

£50 per week over duration of the project for a trainee

Recruitment Costs £650

Local advertising, interviewing expenses and related costs

Tutors Fees £4,800

120 sessions @ £40

Stationery & Printing £2,850

includes cost of designing and printing photographic record and colour reports

Staff & volunteer training £1,580

will include bookkeeping, child safety and road safety

Research Fees & Consultancy £2,400

12 days @£200 over duration of project

Travel & Subsistence £4,500

averaging £75 per week x 60 weeks, includes exploratory visits and volunteers travel costs

Project Management	£5,000
time devoted to project by Director of Education and Director of Finance	
Office Space	£3,000
dedicated space in office for this project	
Classroom Hire	£2,400
60 sessions @ £40	
Insurance	£900
Volunteers Time	£11,250
average 25 hours per week @ £7.50 x 60 weeks	
Outings & Tours	£17,500
@ £1,750 per trip x 10 –based on quotes	
TOTAL PROJECT COST	**£69,155**

<u>CONTRIBUTIONS IN-KIND</u>

Project management	£5,000
Office space	£3,000
Volunteers time	£11,250
Total Contributions In-Kind	**£19,250**

AMOUNT REQUESTED FROM DONOR	**£49,905**

(f) Other Issues

Other questions may be about who will be involved in running the project. This is where you spell out the credentials of staff, volunteers, trustees, consultants and designated project leaders even if they've not yet been appointed.

Often you'll be asked to identify potential risks. Don't be shy to identify them, namely things like child protection, health & safety, accidents, financial overrun and departure of key personnel. They want to know that you have thought about these issues and have taken adequate steps to cover or prepare for them. This might include; health and safety and other training, insurance, appropriate policies, access to professional advice and a contingency in the budget.

(g) Signatures

It's likely that at least two signatories in your organisation will be required to sign the application. One will be the main contact for the project, who will also likely be the person receiving the telephone call and other correspondence, so think very carefully before deciding who it should be. The other person will be a senior contact such as the Chairman or Chief Executive if they are not the first signatory. This is partly to ensure that it's not an application from a renegade employee working on their own as well as for other legal and strategic reasons.

(h) Checklist

Do not complete this in advance. The whole point of this is that you check your application just as you are about to send it off. If used correctly it saves everyone a lot of time. The best thing to do is to appoint a dedicated person with the job of checking and sending off all applications. Perhaps someone in the accounts department or a named trustee not normally involved in the fundraising process.

SECRET #6

Develop, Maintain & Exploit the Database

A database is defined as a *structured set of data*. These days *'held in a computer'* is normally appended to that definition. In reality the address book in your mobile phone is a database, the hastily written numbers in your notebook is a database, the pile of business cards you've collected is a database, all the email addresses you have is a database, and certainly the list of all your previous donors is a database. The problems arise when all these databases are not merged into one, or in a form that is easily accessible and manageable. This means you are wasting a valuable resource and therefore not getting anywhere close to fulfilling your fundraising potential.

Yes, there are manual database systems, with perhaps a rolodex at its heart, that work very well in some organisations, but for our purposes it's makes life a lot easier if it can be computerised. I know that on Windows, Access seems to be popular and as Mac user I've tended to use Filemaker but more recently Daylite.

There is also a tremendous amount of open source software that's readily available that is more than adequate and absolutely free (legally). Links to some of these are mentioned on the Resources page at the end of the book.

I should also mention that we are one of only four UK partners for Daylite software (from Marketcircle) and we specialise in selling and implementing this (Mac only) software to non-profits, SMEs and freelancers.

In setting up any form of database the obvious first question is: Who or what should be listed on the database? The answer is, just about anything and anybody. It's all a matter of how things are organised and categorised and what use you make of it, but you will definitely include existing donors, potential donors, grantmaking bodies, service users, enquirers, suppliers, purchased mailing lists, other charities and even reports, websites and news items that you may wish to refer to.

In the rest of this chapter I'll spell out some fundraising DO's and DON'T's that are particularly relevant to dealing with those contacts (both individuals and organisations) you have on your database. Contacts that you should be constantly updating, validating and soliciting.

Categorise donors

Make sure you categorise your existing donors by the size and type of their contribution. It will define how you deal with them in the future. Make sure that it's very clear who the internal contact is within both your organisation and their organisation (if not an individual donor).

One size does not fit all

Be selective, do not send every request to every existing funder. Doing this risks bringing a large donor down to being a small one. For example if you send a letter asking for people to give £5 per month to your cause a previously large donor may take this option. In their mind they may become satisfied that he or she is playing their part already, and so not respond to later requests.

Don't be cheap with your major donors

In fact major donors should be treated differently to all others. They are a precious commodity and you shouldn't hold back on wining and dining them, giving them an early peak at the annual report and even getting their picture into it. Don't forget that a small percentage increase from a major donor may well be substantial in terms of your overall funding, while losing them would certainly (in most cases) leave a major dent in the revenue.

Everyone's a philanthropist

In my opinion people like to give. Sometimes anxiety, poverty or not wishing to look a fool get in the way. If, as a fundraiser, you begin to think in this way it can make the whole process so much easier. You'll realise that you have the ability to make people feel good about themselves by giving them the *opportunity to be generous*. What a wonderful position to be in.

Start cultivating potential donors from today

Whether institutions or individuals, it often takes time to build a relationship. Use your system to start keeping in touch with potential donors without necessarily asking them for anything. Send them your annual report with a note and an invitation to the AGM. Let them know of your work or projects and ask if they are aware of other people who could benefit. Include them in surveys to find out how your organisation is perceived externally.

Of course if you've followed my advice in the previous chapter and developed a very strong generic fundraising statement, then they will be in no doubt that a donation would be gratefully accepted. It may well be that they take the initiative and approach you with a suggestion more innovative and generous than you might have come up with yourself.

If you don't ask you don't get

A lot of people say that at the end of the day fundraising is about **"The Ask."** Meaning that at some point and in some form you actually have to ask the potential donor for money. True, but by recognising that people want to give, by submitting great applications and by having a well thought out generic fundraising statement you can make the asking so much easier. However, you do have to make sure that your system protects you from asking the same donor twice, unless that's a deliberate strategy.

Remember your manners

"Good manners have never done anyone, any harm," and we all like to be appreciated. Don't leave this to chance. Build in a strategy that thanks donors for their contributions whoever they are and however the donation was received. In writing is always best, but particularly with major donors this should be preceded by a verbal personal thank you from the appropriate person (and *to* the appropriate person)

Sending donors project updates explaining how their funds have been spent is also a form of showing gratitude.

Even if you don't have a specific on-going project you should, from time to time, let them know what you've been doing, Tell them what you'd like to do in the future and let them know (if true) that you'd like to launch a fundraising campaign for that future project, but right now your hands are full delivering on current work. Also don't forget to send them copies of the annual reports, invite them to attend events related to different projects, inform them of press coverage and even tell them about other grants and donations you've received.

The Up-Sell

The person most likely to donate to your cause is someone who's already given. It really is a lot easier to get more money from existing donors than to cultivate brand new ones. This is particularly true if you've remembered your manners as described above.

To take a group of regular £10 per month donors and turn some of them into £25 a month donors is actually a major fundraising project in its own right. In practice I've found that what may happen is that some will increase their regular donation, some will send an additional one-off donation, and some will get their spouse or another relative to start contributing. For this to really work well you need to show the donor how much good has already resulted from their previous donation(s), how grateful people (including yourselves and beneficiaries) are, how great it's been for them (the donor) and how much more can come from an increased contribution.

Of course all major donors should be constantly and tactfully courted in order to either maintain or increase their contribution.

Listen to the donor

When you do hear from a donor, no matter how small, take it seriously. Get back to them one way or another and be clear about the message they are sending. If they are trying to let you know something they're not happy with then it probably means that many other donors and potential donors are thinking the same thing. It could also mean that they actually want to give you more but simply want to know how.

Perhaps your champion inside the organisation is being forced to justify the support you get and is looking for some direction from you, but is not in a position to tell you that openly. However, It could also mean that they are ripe to be approached for some type of corporate sponsorship arrangement.

Remember the fundraising pyramid

The fundraising pyramid is a graphical presentation used to show that in a **major donor fundraising campaign** 80% of donations may come from 10 or 20% of your donors and thus the remaining 20% from 80% of donors.

The actual 80:20 rule is generally attributed to Italian economist Wilfredo Pareto. In 1906 he came up with a mathematical equation to demonstrate the unequal distribution of wealth in his country. However, it is generally taken as a rule of thumb across many disciplines.

Of course in reality percentages vary as nobody ever goes out of their way to actually prove the theory. It's also only by successfully recruiting the smaller donors that the larger ones are likely to appear in any case. However, it is a reminder that a major campaign does need to be broken down into different strategies, aimed at different donors and producing different financial yields, yet all part of the same overall strategy.

The graphic following shows a theoretical £1 million campaign that attracts a total of 1,000 donors and illustrates how that might break down into individual donations. Of course one campaign manager's small donation is another person's entire campaign sorted. So a lot depends on the context.

figure 6: Million Pound Fundraising Pyramid

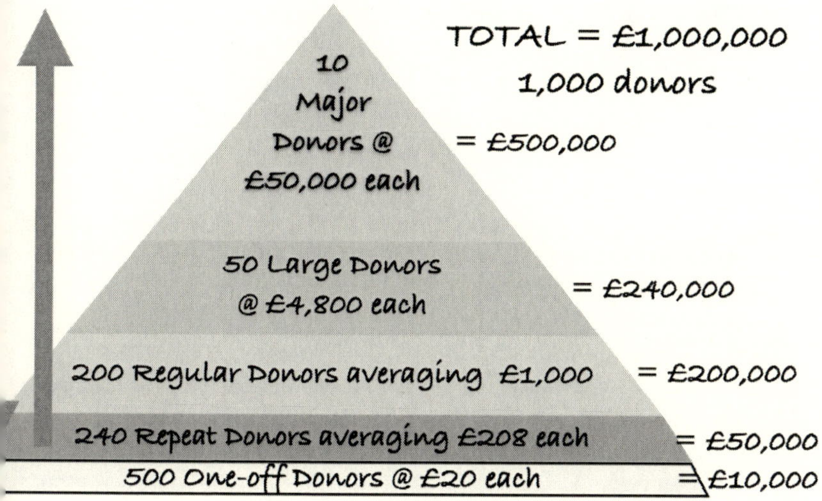

TOTAL £1,000,000

Application refused: Find out why

If you do send in a grant application and for some reason it's refused or declined (assuming it met all the requirements and was well prepared as outlined in the previous chapter) then it's worth getting in touch to find out exactly why. On the other hand, simply getting upset and tearing up the letter isn't particularly productive.

Getting in touch serves two purposes. Firstly, whatever feedback you get will certainly help you improve your future fundraising, Secondly, that funder may think twice about refusing you the next time because of the detailed but mannerly inquisition they know will follow. In many cases the person being spoken to will often let slip some inside bit of knowledge that also gives you that extra edge over other applicants the next time. This information might be related to the size of the projects they tend to favour (despite the published guidelines) or something about the mindset and experience of the people who sit on the actual decision panel.

Find the funding to fit the project (not the project to fit the funding)

I see this phenomena almost every day. People hear about a fund or scheme giving money to help (for example) refugees, victims of domestic violence or out of work farmers. So they hastily try and fit together a project that deals with refugees, victims of domestic violence or out of work farmers. This should be avoided as it only leads to problems. It means moving away from core work and can sometimes even lead to rifts within the organisation. One of the reasons why this happens is often the pressure to maintain jobs within an organisation at any cost.

It is at this time trustees often have to step up to the mark, face their responsibilities and make what might be uncomfortable decisions

However, If you have a project that is, for example, aimed at young people, then there is no harm in emphasizing the fact that **some** of the participants may well be children of refugees, victims of domestic violence or out of work farmers. That's common sense and doesn't compromise anyone.

SECRET #7

Establish the Corporate Profile

I've advised a lot of fundraisers in my time, from experienced high flyers seeking (and getting) millions, down to people wanting a few hundred pounds to take a group of local youngsters on an outing. This means I've also worked with some seriously resourced organisations that fortunately pay well and have a fundraising department most can only dream of. The flip side is that I also get those groups that no one will fund because (to put it mildly) they just don't have a clue. They have an idea, a name and some enthusiasm but unfortunately that's just about it. The question I put directly to most is *"Do you want to build an organisation, indulge in a hobby, or give yourself paid work?"* How this question is answered very much shapes my advice.

I believe there are three common reasons why these newer or smaller groups fail to deliver, or to attract financial support:

- **Lack of capacity** - This means not having the infrastructure in place to do the things you ought to be doing (like managing a million pound budget or delivering services);

- **Lack of a corporate profile** - Refers to all those things that are part of your public image and inspire confidence;

- **Lack of a track record** - The inability to be able to point to previous projects, campaigns or budget to prove that you have the requisite experience to deal with a larger project, donation or grant.

These are the points I will be addressing in this chapter but I'll start by quoting a poem I previously posted on my blog. From the first line you'll realise that I wrote it some time ago, but I thought it was worth repeating here as it contains some good, and still relevant, advice.

> 2009 is now upon us
> So let's make a success of the year
> I wish you success for all your projects and endeavours
> So some advice you must now hear
>
> To start, I will quote from Rudyard Kipling
> He said it so very well
> As soon as I heard it, I got immediately thinking
> This advice, to you all I must tell
>
> "I keep six honest serving men
> (They taught me all I knew)
> Their names are What and Why and When
> And Where and How and Who."
>
> So these are the questions you must answer
> When making the business plan
> These are the things, that if explained correctly
> Potential funders will readily understand
>
> Also, building a team, is absolutely essential
> Don't be tempted to go it alone
> One-man projects rarely reach their potential
> And stay in the twilight zone

Here at DMC we do lots of training
And for you, we'll always go that extra mile
So we advise you to spend some time in 2010
Building your corporate profile

I mean fax numbers, phone numbers, web and email
As well as, how your phone gets answered
I mean office address and dealing with mail
To avoid embarrassing disasters

So I wish you a happy and prosperous new year
That brings you a wealth beyond just money
So my cryptic wish for those with an ear
Is that you get both the milk, and also the honey

I chose to focus on these themes as I believe they could potentially have the biggest initial impact on many organisations, and for many of those who've attended my workshops they've acted as a huge wake-up call in much the same way that the Working Styles and Fundraising Cycle have impacted on others.

Building Capacity

This has to be addressed by what I often call the 'three P's in a pod,' referring to People, Policies and Procedures. The Ps are not necessarily the best words but I like the impact.

People - There are only two solutions to this problem, and that is to either **recruit** or **train**. Recruit people with the requisite experience or train staff or volunteers (including trustees) to the required level. To start the ball rolling you will need to look at the skills of the people in your organisation (perhaps through a skills analysis) and contrast that with the actual skills needed to do the jobs required, which may be administration, accounting, fundraising, volunteer management or service delivery, and of course those things included in the fundraising cycle.

The end result should be a comprehensive training programme and a clear indication of the type of person the organisation needs to recruit. Along with equipment and other capital expenditure these should form the basis of a capacity building bid to an appropriate funder.

Policies & Procedures - By this we mean having in place clear and known methods for dealing with particular situations likely to arise at some point. This may cover the way that you keep records, structure meetings, authorise payments or recruit staff. These policies should be written and made known to everybody involved with the organisation. Just having these policies in place very early on will in itself make things run more smoothly and not leave people floundering around in order to give answers to what should be routine or standard questions.

In my experience, taking the time to develop a policy on the ***'acceptance or refusal of donations'*** will certainly avoid a lot of time and goodwill lost in arguments, accusations and soul searching later on.

Some of the key policies charitable organisations should have in place include:

- Equal Opportunities
- Staff Recruitment
- Child Protection
- Health & Safety
- Financial Standing Orders
- Acceptance and Refusal of Donations

They should be regularly reviewed and those missing added. There should also be a rolling programme of bringing the contents of each policy to the attention of trustees, staff and volunteers. In the UK the NCVO and NACVA have draft documents you can download to help with the development process and links are included on the resources page at the end of the book.

Building the Corporate Profile

Trust comes about through actual transactions whereas confidence comes prior to that, based on perceptions and investigation. Donors want to give to people or organisations they can trust. Trust that they are not crooked and trust that they will get the work done. To a point it doesn't really matter whether you take high salaries or hefty administration costs, they want you to do what you said you would, producing the stated outcomes.

The corporate profile is what inspires confidence and thus paves the way for trust. In looking at these matters we need to be aware where people go for information about a charitable organisation. These include companies house, the charity commissioner, your website, google or Wikipedia and the chamber of commerce. There is no need to delve into each of these as they've largely been mentioned elsewhere in the book. Just being aware of these factors should be enough for anyone to realise they have to keep an eye on and influence the information from these sources as much as possible.

However, more specifically there are some things that come directly under your control. To illustrate my point you need to think about completing the following with your own information.

- Hello...
- Send it to...
- The details are online at....
- You need to speak to...
- I'll fax/email/post you a copy straight away
- You can pick it up from...

The point being made here is that you have to be able to answer these questions being posed or suggested. In other words:

> **"Hello"** means you need to have a telephone number, a name and someone to answer the phone. I'm personally not happy with automated answer phone messages unless as a backup. Phones need to be answered in the name of the organisation. It's possible today to actually own a number that can be re-directed to a landline, mobile phone, VOIP service or personal answering service of your choice, so these things should be investigated. *(I cover many of these*

in various episodes of the Consultant's View podcast) There are also a wide range of telephone answering and virtual office services that are also worth exploring, sometimes described as virtual offices or office angels.

"Send it to" is really saying you must have an official postal address. P.O. boxes numbers just won't do unless used in conjunction with a FREEPOST address for soliciting funds. A private home address may be used, but it may mean spontaneous visits will have to be discouraged. The other option is to actually take a desk in a shared office or have a serviced office through organisations such as Regus (but there are many cheaper local options).

As stated before a **website** has to be seen as essential in this day and age as it is so often the first place people refer to when wanting to know about your organisation or project. Services like Wordpress, although essentially blogs, do let you get a website up for little or no cost at all, with the only real investment necessary being a personalised domain name if required.

You have be able to tell enquirers who they **"...need to speak to"** to ask about a job, to volunteer, to make a donation, to sell you something or even to send you an invitation to a great event. In reality it may well be the same person you refer everybody to for just about everything, but the point is all the people involved need to be clear about this, particularly those answering the phone, receiving emails or opening the post.

As with the telephone you need to be able to not only

receive **faxes and emails** but send them as well. ***Efax*** is a great service for having a fax number but the faxes coming to you as email attachments in PDF type format. Sending faxes will in most cases still require direct access to an actual fax machine.

At some point you'll inevitably get that moment when you've promised to post something only to be told ***"I'm actually in your area all day tomorrow. When and where should I come to pick it up?"*** Working from home is not a problem as people are getting much more used to this concept. However, the room you use should at least have the semblance of an office or place of work. These days coffee shops and hotel lobbies are also favoured meeting places.

Building a Track Record

"The big boys are running off with all the money!" True! Often simply because they can show a track record of dealing with the desired target group, of delivering similar sized projects, of working in partnership and also having friends in the right places...and you can't.

However, there are some legitimate ways to address that and actually develop a track record in the short term. I list some of them here.

Partnerships

Build working relationships with organisations working in a similar field or with overlapping aims. Offer to partner them on bids but also offer to help deliver existing projects which you can then put your name to. Now you can legitimately say: *"We helped to deliver that Very Big project that helped loads of people and had some terrific outcomes"* even if your input was minimal.

Modules
Develop modules, based on the expertise within your organisation, that you can sell or share with others charities as well as private consultants and trainers, to be included as part of their own projects or training programme.

Recruitment
Recruit staff, trustees and volunteers whose track record and experience you can then legitimately claim as being from "within" your own organisation.

Creative Writing
This simply means making the most of what you have actually already done. A bit like a project description for a grant application, these things need to be well thought out while remaining truthful. The trick here is to remember the fundraising cycle and get the right person to do the scripting.

Volunteering
Volunteering as an organisation or individual on other projects allows you to also legitimately add these to your portfolio. It's also a great chance to learn how other organisations and individuals operate.

Permission
Blatantly ask someone if you can claim a connection to a project or piece of work that you admired. This

can be done even if your support was from a distance and may simply have been a verbal recognition of the project or signposting it for your own clients. This is still a legitimate connection.

Conclusions

So there you have it, all seven secrets. My advice is to keep this book on your desk or in your pocket at all times as a reminder and to keep re-drafting those statements.

I'm absolutely confident that whether an experienced professional fundraiser or a newbie just starting out, if you put into practice what is outlined in this book your fundraising effectiveness will improve significantly.

Let's be honest, how can ***building a winning team*** or ***understanding the fundraising cycle*** not be beneficial and impact positively on our thinking? How can an organisation not benefit from spending time ***building its corporate profile*** or ***developing the generic case for support*** to use on their websites and literature and have on the tongues of all their staff and volunteers?

Of course it goes without saying that ***submitting great grant applications, developing and exploiting the database*** and ***diversifying your fundraising options,*** can only be good for fundraisers and the charitable organisations and causes they represent.

However, I know that many of you can still teach me a thing or two about fundraising so please don't hesitate to let me know where I've fallen short and where I've simply missed a trick. Perhap's we'll get some great new material for a second edition, or we can do an interview the podcast. The sky really is the limit.

Additional Resources

Author's website

(http://www.amaldouglas.com)

Anglia Mu'amalat College and
School of Business & Enterprise

(http://www.consultantsview.co.uk)

Consultant's View Blog

(http://www.consultantsview.co.uk)

Charity Commissioner England & Wales

(http://www.charity-commission.gov.uk)

Office of the Scottish Charity Regulator

(http://www.oscr.org.uk)

USA Government Funding

(http://www.grants.gov)

HMRC - Her Majesty's Revenue & Customs

(http://www.hmrc.gov.uk/charities)

GTD - Getting Things Done - David Allen

(http://www.davidco.com)

Colleagues & Associates - Hit List

My Fundraising Methods

Why anyone should donate to my project or oragnisation

Made in United States
North Haven, CT
05 November 2026

21785842R00053